42 Gifts
I'd Like to Give
to You

This is a special collection
filled with wonderful wishes
and the most meaningful
kind of gifts that could
ever be given.

Within the words of this book,
I would like to give
these gifts to you.

42 Gifts
I'd Like to Give
to You

Edited by Douglas Richards

Library of Congress Catalog Card Number: 95-23497
ISBN: 0-88396-420-1

Acknowledgments: This book was compiled by Douglas Richard Pagels. Endless
thanks are given to those who gave me an awareness of the value of these gifts, and
tremendous appreciation is felt for the writers whose wisdom fills these pages. The book
is dedicated to wonderful people everywhere whose quiet generosity makes life more
rewarding for everyone around them.

The following writings by Susan Polis Schutz have previously appeared in Blue Mountain
Press publications: "Go beyond yourself," Copyright © 1976, 1992 by Stephen Schutz and
Susan Polis Schutz. "Sometimes you think" and "You deserve a life," Copyright © 1986 by
Stephen Schutz and Susan Polis Schutz. "As you keep growing" and "We have a choice,"
Copyright © 1988 by Stephen Schutz and Susan Polis Schutz. All rights reserved.

⊓⊔ design on book cover is registered in
U.S. Patent and Trademark Office.

Manufactured in the United States of America
Seventh Printing: March 2000

✿ This book is printed on recycled paper.

Library of Congress Cataloging-in-Publication Data

42 gifts I'd like to give to you / edited by Douglas Richards.
            p.   cm.
        ISBN 0-88396-420-1 (softcover : alk. paper)
        1. Quotations. 2. Quotations, English. I. Richards, Douglas.
    PN6081.A125   1995
    082—dc20

                                                      95-23497
                                                          CIP

SPS Studios, Inc.
P.O. Box 4549, Boulder, Colorado 80306

CONTENTS

❧ The Gift of...

The Gift of Knowing That Beautiful Tomorrows Begin Today

Tomorrow is a beautiful road
that will take you right where
you want to go...

If you spend today
walking away from worry
    and moving towards serenity;
leaving behind conflict
    and travelling towards solutions;
and parting with emptiness
    and finding fulfillment.

If you can do what works for you,
your present will be happier
and your path will be smoother.

And best of all?
    You'll be taking a step
    into a beautiful future.

— Douglas Richards

The Gift of
Good Advice

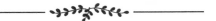

It is a funny thing about life.
If you refuse to accept anything
but the best, you very often get it.

— W. Somerset Maugham

Enjoy when you can,
and endure when you must.

— Goethe

There are times when life isn't all
you want, but it's all you have. So
what I say is: Have it! Stick a
geranium in your hat and be happy!

— Anonymous

The Gift of Being Able to Deal with Your Difficulties

Have you got a problem?
Do what you can
where you are
with what you've got.

— Theodore Roosevelt

I am only one, but I am one.
I cannot do everything, but I can
do something. And what I can do,
that I ought to do.
And what I ought to do,
I shall do.

— Edward Everett Hale

I decided to do more
of what I wanted to do,
stopped doing many things
I didn't want to do, and
gave up worrying about those
things I had no control over.

— Anonymous

The Gift of Setting the Stage
for Good Things to Happen

Find the thing meant for you to do,
and do the best you can.

— Henry Ward Beecher

Don't let life discourage you;
everyone who got where he is
had to begin
where he was.

— R. L. Evans

Let your mind be quiet – realizing the beauty of
the world and the immense and boundless
treasures that it holds in store. All that you have
within you, all that your heart desires, all that
your nature so specially fits for you, waits for you.

— Edward Carpenter

Worthy things
happen to the worthy.

— Plautus

The Gift of a Little Morale Booster

In spite of whatever may happen in your day,
 it's going to be okay.

You've made it through difficult things before,
right? Right. And you always land on your feet.
Maybe not dancing; maybe not always sure about
what to do next. But you always manage to figure
things out. Especially when you're able to keep
your sense of humor and not lose your smile. If
you really think about it, you'll realize that you are
a very strong individual. Someone who may not
have all the answers, but who — at least — is
willing to hope and try and believe.

You can see your way through just about
anything; it all depends on how you look at it.
And when I look at you, I see someone who
really is... pretty amazing.

— Ceal Carson

The Gift of
Using Time Wisely

———— ·⤳⚕⤶· ————

Nothing is worth more than this day.

— Goethe

When I think of how quickly time flies,
I am always sorry that I did not do better
yesterday or last year, because that
particular opportunity will never come
again. But I comfort myself with thinking
that the opportunity to do better next time
lies before me.

— Edward Chipman Guild

I know not what the future holds,
but I know who holds the future.

— Anonymous

Take care of the minutes, and the
hours will take care of themselves.

— Anonymous

The Gift of Believing in Miracles

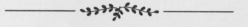

I walk the world in wonder.

— Oscar Wilde

We are the miracle of miracles... we cannot understand it, we know not how to speak of it, but we may feel and know... that it is verily so.

— Carlyle

I am unaware of anything that has a right to be called an impossibility.

— Thomas H. Huxley

The sun, with all those planets revolving around it and dependent on it, can still ripen a bunch of grapes as if it had nothing else in the universe to do.

— Galileo Galilei

The Gift of Being
the Best You Can Be

Sometimes you
think that you
need to be perfect
that you cannot
make mistakes
At these times
you put so much
pressure on yourself
I wish that you
would realize
that you are
a human being —
like everyone else
capable of
reaching great potential
but not capable of
being perfect
So please
just do your best
and realize that
this is enough
Don't compare yourself
to anyone
Be happy to be
the wonderful
unique, very special
person that you are

— Susan Polis Schutz

The Gift of Aspiration

If you can reach out, you can hold on.
If you can imagine, you can achieve.
If you just begin, you can continue.
Search within, and you'll find a reason
    to believe.

If you can get involved, you can make
it happen. If you can give, you will be
rewarded with the taking. If you can
climb, you can climb even higher.
Envision it: your success is in the making.

If you don't put limits on yourself, you
can always keep striving. You might amaze
yourself with what you discover you can do.
If you want to reach out for happiness,
don't ever forget that...

You can go as far
    as your dreams can take you.

— Collin McCarty

The Gift of Spreading Smiles Around

A smile is a curved line
that sets things straight.

— Anonymous

When special feelings come your way,
let them flow into your heart. When
miracles try to find you, don't hide.
When special people come along, let
them know what a blessing they are.

Let your smiles begin
way down, deep inside.

— Collin McCarty

Life is a mirror:
If you frown at it,
it frowns back;
if you smile,
it returns the greeting.

— Thackeray

A smile is the light
in the window of your face
that tells people that
your heart is at home.

— Anonymous

The Gift of Hope

Out of the lowest depths there is a path
to the loftiest height.

When you need some help
to get through the day;
when you need a whole lot less
to concern you,
and a whole lot more
to smile about...
sometimes you just have to remember:

It _really_ _is_ going to be okay.
You're going to make it
through this day.
Even if it's one step at a time.

Sometimes you just have to be
patient and brave and strong.
If you don't know how, just
make it up as you go along.
And hold on to your hope as though
it were a path to follow
or a song to sing.

Because if you have hope,
you have everything.

— Collin McCarty

The Gift of Chasing Your Clouds Away

The greatest mistake you can make in life
is to be continually fearing you will make one.

— Elbert Hubbard

It has been well said that our anxiety does not
empty tomorrow of its sorrows, but only empties
today of its strength.

— Charles H. Spurgeon

Only one type of worry is correct;
to worry that you might be
worrying too much.

— Jewish Proverb

The Gift of
Going Beyond the Ordinary
and Achieving Extraordinary Results

Don't be afraid to go out on a limb.
That's where the fruit is.

— Anonymous

Behold the turtle; he makes progress
only when he sticks his neck out.

— James Bryant Conant

It is not because things are difficult
that we do not dare;
It is because we do not dare
that they are difficult.

— Seneca

If you do what you've always done,
you'll get what you've always gotten.

— Anonymous

The Gift of Moving Beyond Your Misfortunes

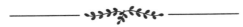

Misfortunes cannot always be avoided.
But they can be made easier — just by
knowing that they will be overcome.

— Seneca

Even though things look cloudy,
they'll get better soon.
Just remember that it's true:
it takes rain to make rainbows,
lemons to make lemonade,
and sometimes it takes difficulties
to make us stronger and better people.

The sun will shine again soon... you'll see.

— Collin McCarty

Every experience, however bitter, has its lesson;
and to focus one's attention on the lesson helps
one over the bitterness.

— Edward Howard Griggs

The Gift of Being Optimistic

Very little is needed to make a happy life.
It is all within yourself, in your way
of thinking.

— Marcus Aurelius

A gentle word, a kind look, and a
good-natured smile can work wonders
and accomplish miracles.

— William Hazlitt

A single sunbeam is enough to
drive away many shadows.

—St. Francis of Assisi

Brighten the corner where you are.

— Old Proverb

The Gift of Keeping Life's Ups and Downs in Perspective

Every mountain means at least two valleys.

— Anonymous

"I've had my trials and troubles.
The Lord has given me both vinegar
and honey, but He has given me
the vinegar with a teaspoon and
the honey with a ladle."

— Attributed to William Bray

If you want to live more, you must master the
art of appreciating the little, everyday blessings
of life. This is not altogether a golden world,
but there are countless gleams of gold to be
discovered in it...

— Henry Alford Porter

If you haven't all the things you want,
be grateful for the things you don't have
that you didn't want.

— Anonymous

The Gift of Real Success

Remember that there is one thing better than making a living – making a life.

— Anonymous

No one can tell whether they are rich or poor by turning to their ledger. It is the heart that makes a person rich. One is rich according to what one is, not according to what one has.

— Henry Ward Beecher

Your outcome in life doesn't depend on your income, but on how you overcome.

— Anonymous

Success is getting what you want. Happiness is wanting what you get.

— Anonymous

The Gift of 24 Beautiful Hours

Everything
is only
for a day.

— Marcus Aurelius

Today you have been given this gift:
twenty-four hours... to spend in the
most beautiful and meaningful way possible.

Let this day be a reflection of
the strength that resides within you.
Of the courage that lights your path.
Of the wisdom that guides your steps.
And of the serenity that will be yours
when this day has passed.

— Jordan Carrill

The Gift of Spiritual Handholds

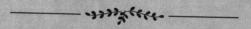

Whatever is to make us better and happy,
God has placed either openly before us
or close to us.

— Seneca

Heaven is under our feet,
as well as over our heads.

— Henry David Thoreau

Our life is always deeper than we know,
and always more divine than it seems.

— James

Life is fragile: Handle with prayer.

— Anonymous

The Gift of Climbing the Ladders That Reach to Your Stars

Even if you can't just snap your fingers
and make a dream come true, you <u>can</u>
travel in the direction of your dream,
every single day, and you can shorten
the distance between the two of you.

— J. Kalispell

It does not matter
how slowly you go
as long as
you do not stop.

— Confucius

As you keep growing and learning
striving and searching
it is very important
that you pursue your own interests
without anything holding you back
It will take time
to fully understand yourself
and to discover what you
want out of life
As you keep growing and learning
striving and searching
I know that the steps in your journey
will take you on the right path

— Susan Polis Schutz

The Gift of Contentment

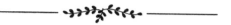

It is not how much we have,
but how much we enjoy,
that makes happiness.

— Charles H. Spurgeon

Reduce your requirements to a minimum.
In that way, you can preserve your independence
and individuality. If you want many material
possessions, you can only get them by selling
your time.... It is not a good bargain. Learn to do
without luxuries and you are free...
rich in sunny hours and summer days.

— Henry David Thoreau

To find contentment, enjoy your own life
without comparing it with that of another.

— Condorcet

Life is ten percent what you make it
and ninety percent how you take it.

— Anonymous

The Gift of Knowing What's Wrong and Doing What's Right

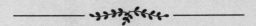

Do unto others as though you were the others.

— Anonymous

It is easier not to begin to go wrong
than it is to turn back
and do better after beginning.

— President James A. Garfield

If I must choose
the lesser of two evils,
I will choose neither.

— Karl Kraus

There is always a best way of doing everything.

— Ralph Waldo Emerson

The Gift of a Life Filled with Love

Love... is the best thing in the world,
and the thing that lives longest.

— Henry van Dyke

Love is something to share with a
wonderful person. And once it's there,
you've got to make it last.
Love isn't something to be taken
for granted. It's something to be
nurtured and cared for and caressed.

Love can last forever... if you want it to.
Love isn't tough and tentative;
it's wonderful and gentle and tender.
Love is mysterious, but it asks that you
keep no secrets. Love is blind, but it
asks that you see how happy it can make
you. Love is more like a flower than a tree;
the wrong things can hurt it so easily.
But the right things can make it more
beautiful than anything else your life
has ever known.

Love is something to be treated as the
best of all blessings, and as your own
little miracle that will keep coming true
...as long as you want it to.

— Barin Taylor

The Gift of a Real Friend

A friend is one of the nicest things
you can have, and one of the best things
you can be. A friend is a living treasure,
and if you have one, you have one of the
most valuable gifts in life.

A friend is the one who will always be
beside you, through all the laughter,
and through each and every tear. A friend
is the one thing you can always rely on;
the someone you can always open up to;
the one wonderful person who always believes
in you in a way that no one else seems to.
A friend is a sanctuary.
A friend is a smile.

A friend is a hand that is always holding
yours, no matter where you are, no matter
how close or far apart you may be.
A friend is someone who is always there
and will always — always — care. A friend
is a feeling of forever in the heart.

A friend is the one door that is always
open. A friend is the one to whom you can
give your key. A friend is one of the
nicest things you can have, and one of
the best things you can be.

— Collin McCarty

The Gift of Understanding
What Others Are Going Through

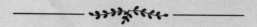

Be kind. Everyone you meet is fighting
a hard battle.

— John Watson

Let us be slower to condemn and quicker
to forgive. If we knew the other fellow's troubles,
we might hesitate to criticize. We might
admire his courage for carrying on.

— A. H. Glasow

Go beyond yourself and reach out to other people
with a sincere love, respect, caring, and
understanding of their needs

— Susan Polis Schutz

The more we know, the better we forgive;
Whoever feels deeply, feels for all who live.

— De Stael

The Gift of Living in a Way That Is Rewarding to You

———— ᴗᴘᴘᴘᴦᴄᴄᴄᴄ- ————

One of the secrets of happiness is to take time to accomplish what you have to do, then to make time to achieve what you want to do.

Remember that life is short. Its golden moments need hopes and memories and dreams. When it seems like those things are lost in the shuffle, you owe it to yourself to find them again. The days are too precious to let them slip away. If you're working too hard, make sure it's because it's a sacrifice for a time when you're going to pay yourself back with something more important than money could ever be. If you're losing the battle, do what it takes to win the war over who is in control of your destiny.

Find time, make time, take time... to love, to smile, to do something rewarding and deeply personal and completely worthwhile. Time is your fortune, and you can spend it to bring more joy to yourself and to others your whole life through. Time is your treasure. And instead of working so hard for it, do what it takes to make it work... for you.

— J.M. Colter

The Gift of Believing
in Your Abilities

If we can put a man on the moon,
you can see your way through
to where you want to be.
There is a way.
There is <u>always</u> a way.

— Alin Austin

Have the daring to accept yourself as a
bundle of possibilities, and undertake
the game of making the most of your best.

— Harry Emerson Fosdick

No one knows what he can do until he tries.

— Publilius Syrus

If we did all the things we are capable of doing,
we would literally astound ourselves.

— Thomas A. Edison

The Gift of Knowing How to Go with the Flow

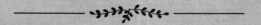

Here is some gentle wisdom that will get you through just about anything: Appreciate, with all your heart, the best of life; do everything within your power to pass the tests of life; and learn how to live with the rest of life.

— Douglas Richards

The deepest rivers flow with the least noise.

— Curt

Cooperation is doing with a smile what you have to do anyway.

— Anonymous

Things turn out best for people who make the best of the way things turn out.

— Anonymous

The Gift of Keeping Up the Good Work

Your gift to life is a thoroughly consistent and beautiful one... You simply present yourself to those around you as one full of kindness and full of sunshine, bringing cheer and glad smiles of welcome upon the faces of all who know you.

You walk quietly and warmly through life, honored and beloved by all who know you, and wherever you have been, you leave people happier and better for your having been with them.

— Edward Chipman Guild

The Gift of a Long, Happy Life

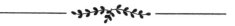

It is magnificent to grow older —
if one keeps young while doing it.

— Harry Emerson Fosdick

I still find each day too short for all the
thoughts I want to think, all the walks I
want to take, all the books I want to read,
and all the friends I want to see.

— John Burroughs

The more sand has escaped from the hourglass
of our lives, the clearer we should see through it.

— Jean Paul

Let every year make you a better person.

— Benjamin Franklin

The Gift of an Angel by Your Side

May you always have an angel by your side ❧
Watching out for you in all the things you do ❧
Reminding you to keep believing in brighter
days ❧ Finding ways for your wishes and dreams
to come true ❧ Giving you hope that is as
certain as the sun ❧ Giving you the strength of
serenity as your guide ❧ May you always have
love and comfort and courage ❧

May you always have an angel by your side ❧
Someone there to catch you if you fall ❧
Encouraging your dreams ❧ Inspiring your
happiness ❧ Holding your hand and helping
you through it all ❧ In all of our days, our lives
are always changing ❧ Tears come along as
well as smiles ❧ Along the roads you travel,
may the miles be a thousand times more lovely
than lonely ❧ May they give you gifts that never,
ever end: someone wonderful to love and a
dear friend in whom you can confide ❧ May
you have rainbows after every storm ❧ May you
have hopes to keep you safe and warm ❧

❧ And may you always have an angel
by your side ❧

— Emilia Larson

The Gift of Courage

Courage is the greatest of all virtues,
because if you haven't courage,
you may not have an opportunity
to use any of the others.

— Samuel Johnson

It is only when
you don't run from yourself
that you begin to get somewhere.

— Anonymous

We have a choice: to spend a lot of time
fighting for what we know is right, or
to just accept what we know is wrong.

We must stand up for our rights
and for the rights of others,
even if most people say we can't win.

— Susan Polis Schutz

If you trust the winner within you,
you will win.

— Collin McCarty

The Gift of Getting Things Done

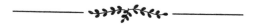

If we are ever in doubt what to do,
it is a good rule to ask ourselves
what we shall wish on the morrow
that we had done.

— Avebury

Begin; to have begun is half the work.
Let the half still remain; again begin this
and thou wilt have done all.

— Ausonius

Ideas are funny things.
They don't work
unless you do.

— Anonymous

An acre of performance
is worth a whole world of promise.

— Howell

The Gift of Lasting Happiness

Happiness is the feeling you're feeling
when you want to keep feeling it.

— Anonymous

The happy have whole days,
and those they choose.
The unhappy have but hours,
and those they lose.

— Colley Cibber

The world has enough sorrow of its own.
For us to add to it would be such a shame.
Sometimes it is difficult, but nothing is sweeter
than balancing out the bad that is beyond your
control with the goodness — and greatness —
that is within reach. Let us always try our best.
May we find our own special ways of making
happiness a permanent part of our lives, rather
than an occasional guest.

— Douglas Richards

You deserve a life of happiness.

— Susan Polis Schutz

The Gift of Making Today Your Moment in Time

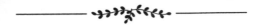

Don't make the mistake of letting yesterday use up too much of today.

— Anonymous

Leave tomorrow until tomorrow.

— German Proverb

Whether you're sixteen or sixty, I encourage you to have the courage to find the magic in this day. Go out of your way to appreciate the deserving things here before you: people who matter, places that will inevitably change, and circumstances that get rearranged all too easily.

Do more than stop and smell the roses. Search them out. Plant new ones in the places you pass by! Send bouquets of flowers to the people you care about. Remember that there's more to appreciate in this moment than we realize...

Years from now, the truth of this will shine. And one of your sincere regrets will be not knowing how good you had it... at the time.

— Douglas Richards

The Gift of Being Patient with the Problems of Life

As a knot appears unexpectedly in a thread, so disappointment blocks the smoothness of life. If a few deft strokes can untangle the skein, life continues evenly. But if it cannot be corrected, then it must be quietly woven into the design. Thus, the finished piece can still be beautiful — even though not as perfect as planned.

— Anonymous

Be patient
with everyone,
but above all
with yourself.

— St. Francis de Sales

The Gift of Keeping Smiles Up and Stress Levels Down

Life is really simple, but we insist on making it complicated.

— Confucius

You don't have to be the one responsible for making everything work. Believe me. The big things are already taken care of: the sun will rise in the morning, the stars will come out at night, and — if you work it right — a child, a love, or a close, dear friend, will share a special smile with you — and make everything wrong... right again.

— Douglas Richards

Enjoy yourself very much, and pack as much health and fresh thought within you as possible.

— George Eliot

There are only two things in the world to worry over: The things you can control, and the things you can't control.
Fix the first, forget the second.

— Anonymous

The Gift of Hanging in There and Holding On

Those who wish to sing
always find a song.

— Swedish Proverb

Consider the postage stamp.
It secures success through its ability
to stick to one thing until it gets there.

— Josh Billings

I will find a way
or make one.

— Anonymous

The difficult we do immediately.
The impossible takes a little longer.

— Charles Alexandre De Calonne
(later used as a slogan by
U.S. Armed Forces in World War II)

When you get into a tight place,
and everything goes against you,
till it seems as though you could
   not hold on a moment longer,
never give up then — for that is
just the place and time that
the tide will turn.

— Harriet Beecher Stowe

A hero is no braver than an ordinary man,
but he is brave five minutes longer.

— Ralph Waldo Emerson

He who has
a why to live for
can bear
almost any how.

— Friedrich Nietzche

When you must, you can.

— Jewish Proverb

The Gift of
Picking Up the Pieces

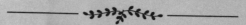

May this be the day when it all comes together ❧ happiness in your heart ❧ serenity in your soul ❧ success in all the things you do ❧ time enough to reach for your dreams ❧ patience to see you through ❧ inner beauty ❧ an open mind ❧ days that find you feeling wonderful ❧ confidence, strong and lasting ❧ strength to do what needs to be done ❧ believing in tomorrow ❧ living in today ❧ knowing the right way is the only way ❧ clearing out the confusion ❧ facing the facts ❧ not being afraid ❧ never giving up ❧ finding hope in hard-to-find places ❧ putting smiles on other people's faces ❧ knowing when to talk ❧ and knowing when to listen ❧ standing by the truth ❧ being firm in your commitments ❧ using your insight to set you right ❧ going from rock bottom to mountain top ❧ learning from mistakes ❧ understanding the greatness within ❧ looking for the good that is always there ❧ sharing the things that need to be shared ❧ remembering that it can all be a puzzle, but solving problems is one of the sweet joys of life ❧ you can always pick up the pieces ❧ and you can always make things right.

— Douglas Richards

The Gift of
a Beautiful Realization

You don't have to know <u>how</u> to sing.
It's feeling as though you <u>want</u> to
that makes the day worthwhile.

— Coleman Cox

Keep on sowing your seed, for you never
know which will grow — perhaps it all will.

— Ecclesiastes 11:6

The Gift of Knowing
That Everything Will Be Okay

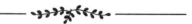

Have patience. Everything
is difficult before it is easy.

— Saadi

Nothing in life is to be feared.
It is only to be understood.

— Marie Curie

The sunrise never failed us yet.

— Celia Thaxter

The Gift of Some of the
Most Wonderful Wisdom of All

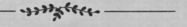

It is never
too late
to be
what you
might have been.

— George Eliot

Beautiful tomorrows
are wished for you...

Beginning today
and lasting
your whole
life through.

— Douglas Richards